Pilar Pallarés

FOSSIL TIME
&
BOOK OF DEVORATIONS

Published in 2021 by
SMALL STATIONS PRESS
20 Dimitar Manov Street, 1408 Sofia, Bulgaria
You can order books and contact the publisher at
www.smallstations.com

This book contains two poetry collections by Pilar Pallarés: *Fossil Time* (*Tempo fósil*), first published by Chan da Pólvora Editora in 2018, and *Book of Devorations* (*Livro das devoracións*), first published by Edicións Espiral Maior in 1996. Her fourth poetry collection, *A Leopard Am I* (*Leopardo son*), published between these two, is also available in English translation from Small Stations Press. For a full list of our poetry titles, please visit www.smallstations.com/poetry

ISBN 978-954-384-113-4

Pilar Pallarés

FOSSIL TIME

WINNER OF THE SPANISH NATIONAL BOOK AWARD AND THE SPANISH CRITICS' AWARD

& BOOK OF DEVORATIONS

WINNER OF THE SPANISH AND THE GALICIAN CRITICS' AWARDS

Translated from Galician by
Carys Evans-Corrales

SMALL STATIONS PRESS

FOSSIL TIME

For Lucía, Ana and Víctor

"There are always two deaths, the real one and the one people know about."
"Two at least," I said, "for the fortunate."

Jean Rhys, *Wide Sargasso Sea*

CONTENTS

By the ruin of reason the word is born
that seeks to return, break the enclosure:
the cork tree, the spurge laurel,
the common laurel, the wild rose-bush,
the camellia, the rosemary,
the cornerstone that began as a bench,
the sandy paths,
the fire in memory
while the sternum of the house breaks.

A femur
dreams of its dog,
that armament of muscle, cartilage
and eyes of mica in the sun.
Humus was made in the vegetable garden,
with cats that killed themselves in large groups
or canker, a domestic hedgehog
and the rooster that the weasel bit
before the second destruction of the valley.
They grind their jaws
and a parietal surrenders to sadness
from the sky above Rañoa and Agrallán.
The skull thinks itself a snake head,
an absent, protective membrane trembling in the REM phase.

The children here never played at finding treasures.
They were the first inhabitants
and this just a land of exile.
Roots: many, it seems,
and strange meteorites or lava formations
from the house receipt.
Also the filigree of the dawn frost
(without yesterday and without tomorrow)
chewing the sprouts.

The fire would have been better
if you had at least been ash the wind scattered
(first swallowing
then dissolution)

Like the quays where you arrive,
exhausted stowaway.
You kiss the earth that blinds your pupil
to produce manure.

Between the breath and the voice,
while life bleeds out at a distance from the peaks
and a furnace is swallowing the entire sea.

(You are still lying:
a harvest of silence,
a waste of echoes,
and you are always outside, on the prowl)

THREE CATS

I stare at them while they stare, caught in a bait: the street.
Hubbub of the city, the sparrows and the doves,
at sunset, the ecstasy of blackbirds
on the Camino. What agreement about nostalgia, among them,
who have no words to nickname fear and sadness?

They saw how the house fell,
how absence climbed the hills of swallowing
and all their recognizable voices vanished.
Worse than the cold and the hunger: abandonment.
How does one unlearn?
How does one forget feeling and the call?
And this pendulum that beats their little brains
and guides the time.

I look at them here,
in the depths of their pupils I discover a sign.
They are becoming used to eating from my hand,
because they know that neither they nor I will return.

(*For Carlos Pereira*)

How do I minister now to your terror
of wounds?
Fissure that suppurates every night.
Each and every one.

THE NEW HOUSEHOLD

We were in an Indian circle bordering the camp.
Armfuls of clothes and baskets,
with few possessions, on our heads.
Apaches in exile: the children.
The dowry of death.

Could I give you my left side?
The hand that dreams
and still holds on to the sky.

(With nothing underneath)

They mistook the time.
The sky will continue spying
over the helpless silence of the animals' skeletons.

Sweeping in silence
still an obstinate wind.

Buzzards are flying over the dismembered landscape.

The voice that I could give has no sustenance.
But I heap up earth, I erect a barrier
so that inside my emptiness grows
and the silence, beating against the walls,
imitates echo and shadow.

We are making an inventory of what no longer exists.
Up to forty-three
from number one,
as if the word carried seeds
(with the stump of her arm)
and below, the obscene stem of a carnivorous plant did not grow.

The gases of silent ignition
(*devious*)
that's where organic matter begins to ferment.
The skeleton of the house smiles,
shaking hands with your howling skeletons
with worms blocking their voices
like the parasites that swelled your bellies as children.

Now the entire world wants to vomit
while the stars cease to rotate
and the gods start to shudder.

(*Ayotzinapa 1*)

Enumerating:
to reach a deal
(but with whom)
on your return.

(*Ayotzinapa 2*)

Lead in the handles?
A fire so fierce it cannot reach me.
Pain requires more subtle materials.

And in every house they entered, each brought their fear
(a fine dust in the bedrooms,
ticks inflaming lungs, soot in the kitchen,
and the wax tears of morning thunderstorms,
when I turned off the radio
and they were motionless in the hallway, spying).
The father was digging,
until he found, beneath strata of frost,
a firm and exempt mineral body,
part of a building being founded
naked as a new Antarctica.
There,
where he would have to learn that nothing grows.

Mounds of earth on spinal columns
and veins of water:
mutilation of the valley
(I know you pretend not to see,
and that to support me
somehow you sustain yourself
in death)

And so to avenge infancy: be a mother to slay a mother.
Lack is a gift that nettles the hands.
I being the one who defends herself, the elm is yours.
The sparks from the pupil come from cold metal,
light from a dead star.
When you appear, I am a mammal's offspring
eager to start walking,
and you are anger.
Do you reject me because there is still another woman, from before,
of whom you see dregs in me?
She doesn't laugh, she doesn't sing,
the flower of the pine tree is fading, scattered in dark caves
that shatter your knees when you scrub,
your mouth if you dare to kiss.

You sever my cord,
and expel yourself.

Your mouth is ravaged.
You teach me the arts of war.
Minor bird
whose bones I chew
at the foot of a fig tree
before nightfall.

The sea is not at such a distance. If I were a dog, I could perhaps smell it behind the mountains, beyond the place where it is interred, where generations of grandparents toiled.

During sunsets one can hear the train in the distance. But this is an enclosed valley. Sweet hills that vanish in the rain; the lower back of Father Xalo, who sometimes looks like a bishop lying down, wearing a tiara worn out by the fog; the forest through which, panting low, a little river that people call River Chan advances.

A monstrous embankment began to devour the lands of Luisito, the nobleman. Soon the palace will be a ruin. The female cats will go there, seeking shelter to give birth. A nest on a branch, between death and death.

The house is growing gradually like fungus on sandy, hostile land. On the slope of a hill that struggled against being farmland and is now a vegetable garden.

First a garden. Facing the *far west* of the valley, overflown by birds of prey, a square area where useless flowers grow, sustained only by beauty, a pure contingency. They don't serve to transport milk, or water. They don't give warmth in bed, they never pay anything. *A surplus in order to progress / in another form of life*. A dream the parents stole from them.

Everything was meant to last. So little.

Cuckoo nests,
all the houses we were repopulating
remain.
Only you, *ab ovo,*
raised in uncertainty,
in the flowering of a dream,
without armaments,
without breastplates,
without seasons weighing on the beams
until they begin to prevail,
flattering and astute,
over the nibbling of the woodworm.

May the land weigh lightly.
On us.

We were shadows in passing,
those who wandered silently over the walls
as the children
closed the shutters,
in an imaginary picture show
(the waves of barley, the strong tide
that traveled in the gentle rain).
Without hideaways for us to lie down
between the chrysalides and the larvae.

Looking from beyond
at how the time and the axe
race along.

The father's skull watches us from afar
– made of love and sadness.
We are a tribe that dispersed,
that wasn't able to continue over generations
until it reverted
into the depths of time.

There wasn't a boat, but I am dying.
There is dark earth under the concrete,
a fossil time.
Insect wings – and a horn that interrupted one's sleep
(you cannot breathe).
In some places the hours slide away,
far from my compasses.
We tried stretching out our arms,
playing with our knees,
a death mask that splits
when it tries to smile
(to remember what it was like).

What do you want from the word's tactile memory
– the brush
of a passing cat
as it leaves a mark of an invisible possession
the orography of a scar that we trace with our fingers,
pores in which salt slumbers
opening and closing like a nocturnal flower under the
fingertips

which knows that the word is always spoken in silence
in waves that radiate from an elusive center
against which stands the index
and its meaning arranges its caution

which advances, blind and mute,
following
the pulsations of the blood
as if they were the echo of an ancient voice
or the footfalls of the wind as it fans the flames

1

Here the non-time (for non-life).
Emerged from childhood,
without stories.
A clumsy learner as an adult,
you bury a piece of china for me
on which a hunter chases a gazelle,
but I don't know how to play alone,
I don't know how to weld the days.

2

Put down roots here,
with the rugged plants?
Only the tip of a hoe that cut through
the treasure chest
the earth doesn't guard.

3

The parents dream of founding,
building next to the house
another form of life
– we are already digging
until we deposit
in the ruin of the past
the disappearance of the future.

What are you after now?
The shadow of another house that sustains our own?

You aren't one of those who walk towards the mouth of the sea,
you don't walk tentatively over a minefield
feeling your blood beating below.
Your pain is useless
among the changes of winter.
It isn't the photo that remained on the floor,
the wounded leg that walks all over Europe,
the open hole in the wire through which a cadaver passes.
Your pain is the first stage of his pain,
an embryonic form,
an initial stratum
over which life will start to sediment
violence and fear.

I take the hendecasyllable upon myself
– the rhythm of my blood,
the silent music of the universe? –
while bombs in bunches erase the harvests
and a highly subtle thread of terror
paralyzes the household animals.

Damn the surreptitious echoes of beauty,
the angels playing by night harps and violins,
the odious obstinacy of hope
fighting to reconstruct us.

And that cleansing of impurity of the word,
their goldsmith capabilities,
the carving of forgetfulness in ivory.

Were we the effect that,
beating against the bodies,
makes the light of a dead star?

Flesh perhaps, now,
if the land accepts us.

Here I am, like a fallen fruit, plunging into an abyss.
The eyelids of earth closed over me
but I still feel them walking in discomfort,
without knowing that I am the deepest stratum
permitted,
a breastplate that wears away and splits,
a lung besieged by stalactites,
a mouth that ruminates a stupid lack of time
in which nothing will be founded.
Brief archaeology:
"bowls,
bones,"
dead dog hair,
lemon-tree leaves.

This summer light
is born of the maladjustment of secret formulas
(the sun is burning so low!)
but the world repeats itself.

Like a body that delays being conscious
of an emptiness in the stomach,
the brain insisting on giving orders
to extirpated organs.

This summer light,
its useless beauty

The house closes its shutters.
The fox curls over its hungry stomach.
Anxious with thirst, the hopping of the queen
opens itself up to tempt the night.

But there is a strange interval between inspiration/
and expiration,
like the worn-down tooth of an antique machine,
a ripped cloth,
a snake that forgets how to shed its skin.

How does it recognize the last time?

The courtesy of death:
that's life,
with a seed of time opening within.

Allow me, goddess,
to extend the hours,
and let the sun continue to enamel the leaves of the clematis
and a path between the fennel
where we will arrange water and food

while a dark voice weaves its stories
cradling the predator's sleep.

Now she dreams of watching over pharaohs
in a darkened chamber

which is the abstraction of onyx
in the abysmal trajectory
of the packaging

the smallest Matryoshka woman
is the key that opens the *iron maiden*

The toe of a giant's boot.
Buckles and straps
and underneath, breathing, the bones.
Forgive me, father, that I still don't pause:
I continue without looking back.
An inhuman force
presses, distends, flattens,
breaks against the cartilages,
changes and undresses me.
Do you feel how cold the frost is?
Or how the dampness of March withdraws, taking great strides?
This is a false ceiling.
The previous one fell down when the beams gave in.
It makes a noise among the rubble,
moaning like a shattered mirror that lost its blue.
River Chan, River Chan
– like a small snake under the tiles,
like an artery digging into the deep,
coming at you
and filling your mouth with blood.

BOOK OF DEVORATIONS

With a foreword by
Luciano Rodríguez

and an afterword by
Miguel Mato Fondo

I'll go into the forest and die where I drop from fatigue. A hunter will mistake my feet for a deer.

The Mahabharata, dir. Peter Brook

Remember, start when you are exhausted, till your eyes can no longer see, they do not wish to see; end that, turn out the light, give yourself over to terrible dreams, abandon yourself to them as if at a ceremony without equal. And at dawn the same, with maximum precision, with the utmost insistence, its meaning feigned.

Thomas Bernhard, *The Cold*

CONTENTS

FOREWORD

ACCOMPANIMENT TO *BOOK OF DEVORATIONS*

1

The first thing that will attract the attention of any reader who comes across the poetic work of Pilar Pallarés (Culleredo, A Coruña, 1957) is her brevity and particular form of expression, which may not please that reader but will not leave him or her indifferent.

Regarding the effect of her brevity, I must be permitted to speak in borrowed words. With a literary work one is not involved with how long or short it may be; writing a little or a lot matters not at all; what is important is having the grace or the gift of "impartial abundance," as the Cuban writer José Lezama Lima would have it in the "Thomist Prayer" of his *Havana Treatises*.

We believe this grace or gift assists and accompanies the author of *Book of Devorations*.

Regarding its particular form of expression and cosmovision, we will attempt in these introductory lines to give a full account of the manner in which the new poetic offering of Pilar Pallarés has been presented.

2

As of today [1996], Pilar Pallarés has written three poetry collections: *In the Dusk* (Castro Editions, Sada, 1980), *Seventh Solitude* (Esquío Collection, Ferrol, 1984), and the one that now brings us together, *Book of Devorations*.

In the Dusk is a collection of somewhat heterogeneous poetry from different times and sensibilities; it is a work of civil-social poems and intimist, improvised singing, which is the one that will increase in the author's later production. The book itself alternates between these two thematic propositions. The (individual and social) hope and despair that appear here become radicalized in *Seventh Solitude*; in this collection of poems there is a conflict between a lack of desire and a lack of love. If in *In the Dusk* there exists the desire (need) to believe in something, to feel the light of the future, in *Seventh Solitude* the solitude and the pain (the two dominant thematic-modulated facets in the book) are entirely assumed; it attempts to arrive at the last grain of solitude, at absolute solitude, total desperation, which is annulled in the achievement. *Seventh Solitude*, a book of love poems, is at the same time a kind of contest against love, intending to attain a state of abstention, annihilation, where solitude and pain – in desperation – are invalidated to give way to an attitude of calm, tranquility, beatitude and assumption of the strange condition that accompanies the human being, an ephemeral being, limited and in transit. As this objective is brought about, it develops the different thematic registers that were already mentioned in *In the Dusk*, later adjusted in *Seventh Solitude*, where superfluous elements were done away with, in order to achieve the "just abundance" in *Book of Devorations*.

3

And on this path towards the text I am attempting to trace, it seems to me almost obligatory to bring to this chapter some of the author's own reflections, substantial and precise, regarding the creation of poetry, the value of the word and her way of understanding poetry. As Pilar Pallarés remarked in 1984 (*De amor y desamor*, Castro Editions, Sada, p. 90):

I write from necessity and pleasure, but I don't live to write. Poetry and life are two voices that accompany and support each other, in an interminable duo of anger and love. At times, one of those voices is quiet, muted so that the other remains brilliant. But I'm not disposed towards either of them disappearing.

Perhaps I create poems to add a little order to the chaos and thus to understand myself and what surrounds me. Perhaps I merely try to give a small margin of eternity to things. In words there remain fixed for ever (an "ever" so provisional in our times) a special light on an August evening, the sweet and violent perfumes of a southern spring, some aspect greatly loved, the abhorrence experienced by those who view certain images of the work done day after day in their jobs.

She says something similar in the *Autopoética, talvez* that she wrote for the anthology *Desde a palabra, doce voces* (Sotelo Blanco Editions, Barcelona, 1986, p. 213), to which we refer the interested reader.

Therefore, in these words it remains patently obvious that writing is her way of being and finding herself: what is written is a possession – freely necessary – since through this she manages to recover those aspects of life, fragments and instants of intensity that would only become passing experiences of life, limited to a finite time of not being able to eternalize the word. What is lived is eternalized in the actualization of the poetic word that each person creates in the act of decoding what is read.

After establishing the presuppositions with which this author writes, it is much easier for us to involve ourselves in the scope of the word ciphered in messages.

4

In *Book of Devorations*, thirty-five poems of small-to-medium extension open up to us another – new? – poetic proposal by Pilar

Pallarés. From despair, from negation of love as a consolation-refuge that was the coin of *Seventh Solitude*, the poet emerges reinforced-comforted in the face of a new conception, having passed through the hellish fires of desperation, where one can see that she purges the elements responsible for her dejection. Purified, she enters another route in which time and its marks on the poetic I, the means and the habitable spheres, create the themes of the keys to *Book of Devorations*.

The desert, the emptiness, the wounds of different kinds, the marks of deprivation, repeat themselves over and over again.

What is it, then, that changes regarding the previous proposition? The ephemeral condition of the human being has already been accepted, and this step causes the positive aspect of life to be seen with less negativity – or more realism. It's true that living is dying, but not everything dies: look at its handholds, look at the plank that saves the world as it decomposes. All that is saved from the shipwreck are objects, minute marks of life, shadows of what was once life's plenitude.

I think that what most defines this poetry is the belief in the word, a fact that creates and provokes a new vitality in the poetic protagonist, who is negative about herself and given to all failures, which leads her to be born again, to initiate the path once more, like a wave coming to die on the beach but then incorporating itself into the mass of heavily salted water and beginning the movement anew:

I am reborn in the watery limits
between the shadowy word
and the terror of abandonment
I rise from the mother that still nourishes me
from this dark silence that drinks me
and avoid myself in a sensitive thread
within a stream of acrid salty lava

[...]

I become reborn and reinitiated
and I reinvent within me a tide without truce
and recreate myself in mud
in a star of acidic hot blood
in this nuptial fear   in so much mistletoe

I return to myself and torment myself
and tell myself that I am
that I have a name
an initial of light
a scarlet letter that signals my brow for the gods

There exists in *Book of Devorations* a manifesto of life which is resolved in a resigned affirmation of the sad human condition: let yourself go, live your days knowing they are counted, that the winds pass and return only to pass again, that the sea of life endorses and detracts, "and let what lived before fall into oblivion," according to a line that ends the first poem of the book, well titled, we believe, as "*ars vivendi*." That which was alive yesterday falls into oblivion, and the word thus used continues to live through death while still alive.

We find in *Book of Devorations* an apparent contradiction: that which is lost is what is saved, thanks to the word of important individuals, a voice prolonged in the verbal temple, thus creating a "liturgy without gods" that provokes in the poetic protagonist a state of beatitude, tranquility and purification, a state of grace not exempt from certain mystic tensions.

From the point of view of verbal temporality that predominates this collection of poems, it is worth drawing attention to the frequent use of the present indicative and the infinitive, zero time and permanent action becoming real. This is nothing but another form of reaffirming oneself in the actualizing power of the word: a changing and unalterable photograph of the past-present so that it will always be an eternal future. The poet thus being the person who comes back to give words to "things" as things and not "objects," echoing in the naming of them the living, eloquent vibration of Being in things. The echo of silence of those who are filled, as Hugo Mujica would have it (*La palabra inicial*, Trotta, Madrid, 1995, p. 46).

5

The measured writing, the condensation, the necessary word taken to its limits, the lack of conformity and the resignation, the lack of silence and the broken verse, the tension in the bite of the tiger that becomes silken after acceptance, are aspects to bear in mind in her work: poetry that aspires to recover the metallic echoes used in the voice, so that it continues to vibrate.

Pilar Pallarés is the same type of poet as Rosalía de Castro, Emily Dickinson, Virginia Woolf, Sylvia Plath, Florbela Espanca, Alfonsina Storni, Alejandra Pizarnik, Clarice Lispector, Cristina Peri Rossi or María Mariño.

And that is no small achievement.

Luciano Rodríguez

at times there remains a single broken statue
in which the weather gathers damp roses
and an ill-defined flower from seasons of snow

make no effort to recompose the line of your smile
don't search in your shoulders a warmth that disappeared

allow the night to blind your white brow
so smooth in old age, so well-preserved still

let the larvae and the ants devour your eyes
and let what lived before fall into oblivion

(*ars vivendi*)

In the evening, with a dog and a book
half-open
I sit on a knoll in the garden
and pause to contemplate the passing of life.
From the east flies in a timely flock of birds
which I cannot identify.
There's an uneven light covering the landscape,
there's a fragile, cautious
winter light.

The heart listens, and, at times, insinuates a question.
There's a mantle of calm stifling shouts,
hiding desolate features.

Is this life? This pernicious pain, advancing
through underground channels?
This
        mediocrity?

In the evening, I contemplate the fictitious calm and wait for
                                                                                                    delirium
while the dog, the book, the timely flock of birds,
an echo of a thunder-clap in the very far distance...

and when the time comes for memory I hate you
and return to my mother's house   your face
is a fragment rescued from the Garden of the Hesperides

an army deserts my fingers
installs its drums in my blood
ventures into scum

on the east side the evening horizon fell to pieces

mother   similar to the spume of his sex is that of vengeance
have pity on me who lies to the left of the bed
with hunger for his mouth and his spittle
and an ivy in my stomach

mother   make me a crown of diminutive teeth to bite me
have pity on me
who was detained by God's sword at the door to Paradise
and walks lost   with nostalgia for his acid tongue and wax
on my waist
bereft of the initial syllable of all words
and already so given to death

mother   tell him that the warrior
taught me how love and hatred grow from the same earth
and thus in hatred I love and in his body I wait

mother   tell him to besiege me
and let the price of his hostage be very high

to unleash his dogs
and let them devour me

never enter   remain prowling
be a tiger injured on your trail
an insect of light circling you
destroying my wings   burning me in silence

never enter   remain on your ribcage
growing for you   branching out
in lanceolate leaves   in bleeding crowns
dispersed by a malevolent wind

never be slothful
be the tide
vibrate in bird

fall asleep in the night of your hair
in the sharpness of your lip diminish
be barely pigment in your skin
phosphorus burning in the center of your bone
be dispossessed
be you
in the muscle that tenses your thighs
in the vein that turns blue on your wrist

the lips of the drowned woman
her breasts slashed by the fishes
such things   fragmented images
this salted flavor in her nipples
your mauled arms
the coral

what the price of your possession?

I will resist:
when the years go by
and impart to your body the appearance of ingratitude
I will penetrate the citadel
amid the flying dust and the silence
and in the devastation
I will kiss your pubis
the folds of your mantle
and your sleeping mouth may perchance respond to me

it will be a rumor as sad
as a caress on the shattered torso of a statue

what's left of life is this earth-bound place
chewed by worms
bitten by the tiny teeth of the mole
swept by the north-east wind
and where the forget-me-not lies
and the meaty roots wrap around your body
penetrating your eardrum and your hair
they weave a threaded veil for your empty eyes

what remains is the inconstant nervous hum
of a distant factory
and the vain ostentation of funereal flowers
and this mute ritual in which you abandon yourself
to the laborious soil and the profoundly secret quest

while we descend in silence to the sea shore
and a huge March sky trembles over the world

here I leave my knowledge
written in illegible letters
which time will destroy
or perhaps a fragrance will arrive late
in this space that I color   with kissing and salting
and a non-existent person will recuperate me
with my errant history
and all I lost and never had
and from the yellowing purple silence
you still emerge
my deprivation
my bitter suppurating bone
my thread of hidden enemy blood
membrane of my inner ear
fossil of my flesh
my temple

Life imitates cautious geometries
and in the silent evening
your eyes pass again through aridity, the distance
between lips and shadow,
the rectitude of margins, the basalt of years.

But come into the center,
debate with me in the crack, in the interstice,
and at the deepest level
seek the wellspring,
the vein of white gold.
Mark with your index finger a name in the stone.
Baptize me with it:
I baptize your youth with salt
and I choose from the alphabet a letter in blood,
a serpent and a clover.
Hold me in a murmur
and listen to the swallowing in the belly of the whale
of your flesh and mine
and how life flows between rancor and ire
and lust devastates the angles of our mouths.

Geometrician of wires, a bird hops about.

ask the day for the sun that warms your face
the ululation of the wind in its highest terraces

the beauty of bodies has angles that ache

heart: do not move

Now the spring will begin its development,
covering itself with the exuberance of other bodies
and a new desire that you confuse with love.

In the stagnant waters where an insect vibrates,
in the light that the evening directs from the cane-fields,
in the anguish of the ivy on the wall,
there, oh sleeping woman, oh pallid and forgotten,
her insanity awaits you, the bowl of her lip.
Her tender salted tongue causes her ankle to slip,
designs a thread of silver and blood around her foot.
C'est le venin du temps,
the remorse of the days when death was a guest
to whom you gave your flesh, dark pink of the breasts
lost forever.
Today you are injured by the presences of the life you do not live,
bodies you disdained, eyes of deep water
in which a ring gleamed, without on passing by
your even noticing, given over to the chess game
of not-being, or barely being
the echo of a silence.

Now the spring will begin its development...

But nostalgia and hell are worth nothing.

tomorrow I'll wake up, and will I be alive or dead?

let nothing from the past convene around me
and let nothing assist me at this hour
in which a blended body is born from my shoulder blades
let nothing recognize and recollect
the little girl I once was, touching crystal
so that another water is lost and yet another,
and let no pious person place a veil over my eyes
so pallid at night
let nothing I love be conceded to me
so that one hunger is devoured in another
and another mouth continues to my center
where there are clay children that refuse to grow

let the deflected light return, and not save me

and again going out to the dawn streets
stepping on a rose with a delicate lung

here I am   father   gently weeping
– the day has dawned rusty –
I want neither your eternal bread nor the joy of the chosen
I disdain the acid wine that you offer me
at the hour of consolation   in the slowly measured rite
pardon this silence
pardon the life of the son that was born when my blood flowed
and my mouth was adept and firm to the caress
I now dwell here   in this portion of the abyss
and never a call when I return home
– my son made of teeth and neurons
like an arborescent engraving on the wall
my son   with his neck so frail
and the indecision of sex
like an abstract design on the wall –
in that time   in that blood you gave me
in that knowing I was upright over the center of the world
a line of shadow preserved my eyes
I now dwell here   before the one I never knew
fortified in me   abandoned by the angels
with my clotted blood identical to itself
recognizing in me all the orphaned life
daughter of the mother that I was   sister to my death

this room   the walls
the silence
at the other side is the tiger   its claws
destroy the varnishes
scratch a still-living muscle
I say tiger and the syllables fall down
the scent of your balsam falls into the room
the note so extinct in this psalm
oh my beloved beast
curse me
make me whole
swallow me
satiate yourself in me

Some ingenuous consolation at the end of this age
feigns that life still reserves features
we dare to love, echoes of certain voices
that return from the past, and the salt from other rivers.

But today I'm reading the naked pages of what I have
and in the balance commands the weight of what I lose,
the lunar substance to which the evening submits.
Just one street of statues, a silence of parks
amid blinded eyes. There where the nettle grows,
and the inflammation of mouths,
where the March rains
ferment new bodies for death.

Born of a pleasant river, exposed to chance and to mutation. For you to sustain me, what thread keeps you identical to your image in November, goddess of water, city given over to the cycle of departures and returns?

When I return, will I recuperate? Or is it only you who stays, made of stone and calcium, outliving me?

If I open the doors of my house, the past classifies its choir of voices and its fruits: exhausted multitudes descending toward the quays, sick light of the evening on the ladder against fire.

When I return, will I recover you? I bite the flesh of the hour to have you, this space of shadow and vestiges.

In your silence stagnates the flower of the season.

(*Lisbon revisited*)

ARLESIAN

Maybe the doves sensed your presence and came to you.
It's so strange to you, this silence,
this calm of your being in which the day stretches and falls
asleep...

Invisible lions watch over the passing of hours and cadavers
through these gentle waters.
But something in the air still reminds us of farewells and
accordions
and the hoarse intimacy of port cities.

The photos of Man Ray in the museum's halls
and an open window to the Roman baths,
with the twitching of insects and a tired beating of wings
in meandering light. Amid your varied paintings
the sexuality
of a sleepless
woman
spies on us without eyelids
and horses are dying in the circles of chalk.

(*Designs by Picasso in the Réattu of Arles*)

(In the Alyscamps, Arles)

Porous substance in the morning,
imbibed with light,
fructified with the color of terracotta.
Without an affiliation,
without a name.
Devoid of signs and history
to be only the one who contemplates,
the one offered for every possession
and rapture.

. . . .

During the entire hour, the absence.
In the blue and ochre plenitude of these metallic fusions
an empty space in the soul,
a desire to be confusingly
mineral and epidermic,
to entirely empty myself like a sarcophagus,
"*dulcissima et innocentissima*,"
old, small death, Chrisogone.

. . . .

To empty myself of being in order to be everything
by chance at every instant.
Devastate the past.
Wrench and polish until you touch the center
of hardness, the essential bone structure,

the nucleus of my nothingness.
To be space and surface.
To let the seasons of silex and anthracite
extinguish the heat from my mouth,
every bird forget me.

. . . .

A site of privation.
Not even the whirling dust of your bones,
the coin that this abode pays you,
the artillery of a crustacean that traveled
amid the folds of the tunic
along the course of the waters.
All that remains of your age is this silence,
this worn-out stone it was unable to guard for you.

. . . .

At the end of the emptiness is your name.
At the end of my nothingness comes the night
with its ferocious vagaries.
Something, which never ceases, sings as it passes by,
leaves a sharp note in memory of blood.

thus it is and thus it will be
while I hurry through this immense evening
and a sundial lies to me at five-fifteen

the weight of what I lose?
the absent feeling of stone?
simulations of the light
watching over the still body of the chrysalids

this hour never passes:
it moves to a more diffuse border
fatigued and gasping   it bites the beginning of the wave
waits in the belly of the whales
drags sand and whiteness
returns eternally with the violet hair of drowned women
with my features now pale for some twenty-odd years

the weight of what I lose?
the gravitational law of what I gain
in the denser waters of this hour
in the refuse of what I was and what is now poured over me
and allows me to drown among my dead

memorized clay figures
all and nothing
mirages of salt that the evening invents

I am reborn in the watery limits
between the shadowy word
and the terror of abandonment
I rise from the mother that still nourishes me
from this dark silence that drinks me
and avoid myself in a sensitive thread
within a stream of acrid salty lava

and I shout at myself and beg myself
for a nocturnal flower growing from desire
a tiger's claw that now couldn't care less
and plays on my nerves

I become reborn and reinitiated
and I reinvent within me a tide without truce
and recreate myself in mud
in a star of acidic hot blood
in this nuptial fear in so much mistletoe

I return to myself and torment myself
and tell myself that I am
that I have a name
an initial of light
a scarlet letter that signals my brow for the gods

I return to my sinews
to this solar sphere which winter wafts away
to a bronze idol covered in fungus
to a spiral whose health is disguised
for my hunger

COSTAFREDAN

Imperceptibly I think of your body,
a labyrinth of metal.
It makes my life tender
with its habits learned as a widow,
but who will save me if I am my own trap,
if it is I who must cut off the ears of the stag,
and who will search for me
if your finger expelled me from the human world
to throw me into myself,
if you profaned the tomb of the queens
and the sun's ray tore me to pieces
and wrenched the bandage hideously from your lip.

Burning was necessary,
living not so much.

From you to me a hesitant line.
Your voice on the telephone
and an invisible life, a terror that silence
releases,
adheres itself to the ribcage
– a tongue of fire,
a tepid animal that never leaves me –
and I suffocate from not screaming,
and from not singing, not subsisting,
still not discovering, still not always.

A glove without a hand,
a heart that I turn inside out
and it has naked veins,
violet nodules, small misplaced brown eyes.

I open-close my display of mail,
set out each marked letter.
I obey, I obey.

Misery.
And sometimes the brilliance of lightning,
the body gently obeying
the gravitational law of other bodies,
the insistent call of the universe.

But in the end it's always an inner structure,
fleeing with no voice, no hands, obscenely,
finding and losing, and making mistakes.
Time runs out. And the sun's ray no longer warms,
the heart resumes the country dance
with an error at every step. A sound
dissolving in a sea of mercury,
a crevice of light that the wind abates.

At the end, only words.
A weight too light for such a long season,
a huge sad addition that never covers the harvest.
Words gathered together for the dowry of the dead,
glass beads, deteriorated coins, fennel,
pebbles to mark one's routes to goodbyes.
A sailboat on unplowed land,
a flourishing of tides, waves losing strength
towards where?
I impart words to you,
little fruits to reduce the pain.
I present you with a handful of earth from the river
so that within it the light rain and its aroma
do not allow you comfort,
so that a benign god is moved
by the saliva of the nostalgia on your lips,
by the strange substance of human passions,
and orders your return.

(*For Antón Avilés de Taramancos*)

WITH ANTÓN AND MY FATHER IN THE SAME SHADOW

To fathom words spoken to you
it's essential to dig in a dark well
until you beat your entrails.
In them you float with my father's shadow,
his May lost in your March,
locked in a time that excludes me
and walks the calendars endlessly backward.

A sword prohibits me that reign,
thrusting my body to the light:
that of a pious angel
honing the blade with the voice of blood,
prattling with passion:
the law of life,
the one that raised you against the Beast
and gives birth to you on the grass, wing of a goldfinch
liberated in April from mistletoe and mud,
dew of the morning, murmur of soft rain,
fire and root, Antón,
where you still live,
where the bones of my father pasture lambs
in the breastbone of the season of blossoms.

Suddenly my silence returns,
the one from before the one before,
that existed in me when God was not yet born
and the world was a doubtful creation
on the borders of non-being.
Neither the squealing of seagulls
nor the somnambulistic horns talking of other seas:
the fury of the humans fell over us,
threw into the river its greed.
I am not afraid of death:
I learned to make it mine and turned it into a ritual.
I am accustomed to the creaking of bones against the rocks,
to the dying gasps of the fish I feed to others,
to the blood that tints me in shipwrecks.
I know I will resurrect:
my stomach will swallow this bitterness,
it will bring about ruin in new life
and I will return supported by the tide,
in the steps of a dance I've reinitiated
since time began.
Now I atone for the error of men,
I pay for their failings with my pain
and make ready my vengeance: this silence,
this desolation, its solitude.

(*"Aegean Sea"*)

ART OF THE CAT

Look leisurely at the world from afar
because you arrived at dawn,
you captured its essence
and it was dispossession.

But at times the world takes the form
of this morning sun that warms the muscles,
of this maternal sky that softens you:
give yourself to ecstasy for today,
submit to this siege,
behave as if life called the play
and maintains the visage of God.

Indolent and haughty,
epicurean
and skeptical,
contemplate emptiness in its multiplicity,
do not desire anything
and do not love,
because love is a fiction, anguish a song
in which the sirens erred,
because if you love, you will be abandoned.

Let the waters pass,
and the armies,
and one more day bow under the weight of Hercules.

Only a slight breeze pimples your flank,
distends your pupil.

The fascination of not being.
Seated on the roof, you let the days go by,
only managing to love the light's decline,
a trail that leads nowhere.
Am I speaking of you or of me?
I confuse sexes and persons,
I destroy the seasons with two blades on the sword,
I have bifrontal features,
two clay mouths that kiss me and that I kiss
to reach in me your absence,
to fear you in me and not to flee.
How strange it is that I can feed myself
on your privation,
that my everything can be done with your nothing,
that your death lives in me
and in your refusal to be
I am me.

I have already been here
this same sadness once owned me
this desolation idle and silent
like a sleeping mollusk
I already was, had already been
swallowed one day by identical waters
still there to make death denser
death yet again
small muzzled
knot of coral and tongue still vibrating
of blood
still
nourishing itself on me
for what there may have been in me of bravery and firmness
oh time time death
umbilical cord that strangles me
and eros of liquid eyes
consolidating their truce
so I will be a traitor to myself
in this deaf and somber country
to which everything returns
nation to which I give myself
like an exhausted hostage that nothing will save

what there may have been in me of bravery and firmness
that raised me counter to the current
Venus resurrected
dark nursing mother gathering the fragments
restoring my body
– a broken wing, a sinuous breach
tainted with rust
duplicating me –
so that I give myself once more in offering
to the initial silence
to the first shudder before the scream
that rebuilds me and turns me into rags
and raises me like a wall against time
encircles and arms me and can do nothing
against the forms of time
its perpetuity
its tumult

— VARIATION 1 —

I neo-romanticize
while life heals the wound it gave me
and I am woken by a thirst I didn't have
a longing for channels and wells
where floats a voice that the wind rips away

for this deficiency there were never words
for me there were only gifts of
conformity and determination
permanence and being
for which I was sister to the fern and the otter
and the world interrupted its questions

I'll go into the forest
and live

– VARIATION 2 –

pour que je n'erre pas comme une égarée
autour des troupeaux de tes amis.

do I fight between two commands?
I survive
silently in the cycle of cryptograms
in the obstinacy of the mole who doesn't know
she will never see sunlight

my animal self stems from the will
my human aspect
rejects the instinct for reconciliation

my animal self forgets and perseveres
munches on the tender grass
rests around it
drains the water of this thirst from the stream
from the evening wind the calming of this anxiety
and falls asleep in confidence
sure of a voice to discover and clutch hold of it
to replace the horseflies
and take it home

my animal self does not fear the winter

"As I arrange these verses and these days."
As if an invisible thread organized the chaos,
the secret music of the stars
sustained the universe
and I were no longer human:
    just one more creature,
unconscious and lascivious,
trying out a dark trail that always leads to God.
As if I were God, the day worker
who attends to the fields, prunes the lemon tree
and subtracts pain from the world like someone scraping a
mountain.
    As I arrange these days, these verses.
As if the same were the word and the act,
muteness and not being.
As if a single syllable stolen from silence
justified life
and maintained the wheel of time on its axis.

In the splendor of the hours
I am the seated scribe
and I wait for the day to forget
on my slate
a diagonal straight line, the face of an ephebe,
a touch of blood and spices,
the perfume of sagebrush,
the magnetized thighs of a woman dancing.

Unable to deal with life,
I transcribe what exceeds me,
I concentrate on guiding lines love and its detritus,
the contraction of mouths in bed and in battle,
the pupils of cats.

May the gods forgive my renunciation
of the torrent of existence:
I permit the waters to fall between my fingers
and my youth,
and while I dilapidate my minutes
I retain other stories,
I gather the attention of other cadavers
and to their precarious members I give the shape of the eternal.

Perhaps one day in the future,
when the jaws of time
have devoured my flesh
and that of the worms of my flesh
and the following generation,

someone will wipe away the dust on my slate
and in the extinguished brilliance of its signs
decrypt me,
to discover that I was the ephebe and the damsel,
the warrior's helmet,
the root of the sagebrush,
the feline's thirst,
the chrysanthemum.

AFTERWORD

THE LUCIDITY OF THE SCRIBE

Of those poems that we have read there remain verses that, in a mysterious and sometimes impertinent manner, seek a place in our memory, a corner from which they toss from time to time – also in a mysterious and impertinent manner – their carefree light to form part of our own words. If I now had to remember some of them, those from "When the raptor comes" would be an admirable choice:

I passed for a while around things,
they passed atrociously over me

which would be followed by those others in concert, no less beautiful and sad, devoid of hope and testimonial:

I will perhaps be a little lonely,
all sad as the evening falls,
saying farewell to the paths

These verses belong to *Seventh Solitude*. So many years after its publication, the latest poetry collection by Pilar Pallarés, *Book of Devorations*, with such a significant title, written with an unhurried rhythm that corresponds to the Horatian calling of the author, grows and expands previous lines, but perhaps highlights the intention to free itself of many of the external references, objects, places, scenes, that populated its old solitudes, so as to center its discourse on the reflection on common themes. Poetry and life, those "voices that accompany" in an interminable "duo of rage and love," as the poet herself has written and some of us tend to repeat, in which, at times, one of them is mute so that the other can shine. The other themes are writing as possession, the misshapen footprints of time, an existential and reflexive backdrop before life and the reflection on writing and art, which do no more than enhance that existential and uninspired, or pessimistic perhaps, both cultured and experiential vision, without wishing to place too much attention on any one in particular, so characteristic of Pilar Pallarés.

Another difference that we observe and should consider in contrast to the previous book is that related to its structure. At that time the juxtaposition of poems that frequently presented titles was more obvious. Now the new book becomes more organic, in a vertebral line with symmetrical poems. Even the titles of some of them, if there are any, appear placed in irrelevant positions, so as not to detract the spotlight from this vertebral system.

In this second edition of *Book of Devorations* [2009] a new poem has been added, also dedicated to Antón Avilés de Taramancos. I say "also" because another poem appeared in the first edition, beginning with the inscription "At the end, only words," which leads us to the aforementioned reflection on writing. This second poem, titled "With Antón and My Father in the Same Shadow," has a certain Cunqueiro air, close to poems from his book *Herba aquí e acolá*, precisely in that brief reference to rebirth in a splendid April:

> *the law of life,*
> *the one that raised you against the Beast*
> *and gives birth to you on the grass, wing of a goldfinch*
> *liberated in April from mistletoe and mud,*
> *dew of the morning, murmur of soft rain,*

There has been discussion in contemporary poetry regarding the thematization of disenchantment, like the remains of the romantic accent that in some poets would explain a certain weariness or deception, or even a certain disillusion. A painful vision of the world, perhaps. The poem "In the evening, with a dog and a book," which we already knew, since it had been published in the first volume of the anthology *De amor e desamor* (1984), sits well with the sensitivity of this new collection. It contains a reflexive tone with a strong elegiac mood, especially in the poem dedicated to Avilés, but also the feeling of someone who knows in advance and understands the answers to the questions. Life is, effectively, what occurs at that precise moment, the anecdote that is not going to change the panorama of fallen horizons. The expression of that false calm that produces screams, an evident manifestation of the anguish in the painting "The Scream," seems to reveal the presence of the tortured world of E. Munch, that infinite howl:

The heart listens, and, at times, insinuates a question.
There's a mantle of calm stifling shouts,
hiding desolate features.

Is this life? This pernicious pain, advancing
through underground channels?
This
        mediocrity?

Related to this, the poem "Art of the Cat" expresses from the feline's pupil a vision of life as abandonment and futility. Hence the reference to a desired and yet impossible distancing. So contrary to the one who asked, in previous verses, without hope or perplexity before life's mediocrity:

what's left of life is this earth-bound place
chewed by worms

bitten by the tiny teeth of the mole
swept by the north-east wind
and where the forget-me-not lies

[...]

while we descend in silence to the sea shore
and a huge March sky trembles over the world

Concern for the remains of life that takes us to another theme, the presence of the statues, those "torsos broken by time" as Cortázar has said. "*Ars vivendi*," the first poem of the book, leads us, in its oblivion, from the *broken statue* to the scribe of the last poem:

at times there remains a single broken statue
in which the weather gathers damp roses

This is also present in the poem "the lips of the drowned woman": lying down like a statue. And then like the last word of "what the price of your possession?":

it will be a rumor as sad
as a caress on the shattered torso of a statue

As the poet González Garcés, a friend of many of us, has written, in Pilar's poetry there is a desolate intimism, a serene anguish regarding time, a deaf rebellion before the pain of the world and its mediocrity in the monotony of days and events, all captured with fine sensorial perception.

Book of Devorations ends with a great poem, possibly one of the most lucid texts in our contemporary poetry. The one we would like to name "The Scribe," despite the fact that the woman who wrote it didn't give it a title of any kind. The reading of previous verses sends us constantly towards it, announcing it:

here I leave my knowledge
written in illegible letters
which time will destroy
or perhaps a fragrance will arrive late
in this space that I color [...]
and a non-existent person will recuperate me
with my errant history

The last poem, therefore, is presented to us as a text-guide, in which the desire for transcendence and the reflection on writing are its master lines, considering also the role of art in overcoming time and death. The anxiety of the artist is to dwell in the eternal. Aesthetic hope (continuing with Cortázar) which is nothing more than the hope of being. In this sense, in Luciano Rodríguez's prologue, which illustrates the collection perfectly, the importance of writing as possession, within the concept of art as transcendence, is highlighted. But there is something more in this poem, which leads us to a question with a difficult answer: what is the poet's, the scribe's, purpose, and what does "I transcribe what exceeds me" actually mean?

May the gods forgive my renunciation
of the torrent of existence:
I permit the waters to fall between my fingers
and my youth,
and while I dilapidate my minutes
I retain other stories,
I gather the attention of other cadavers
and to their precarious members I give the shape of the eternal.

There is the reflection on writing, on that particular scribe as well. It insists on the purpose of writing. The word that transcends, like art. Let us look at the poem: the lines on the slate. Let us make a reading that works with other poems: "Head of the Goddess in My Hands" by Antonio Colinas, "*Portrait of a Man* by Antonello da Messina" by Álvaro Cunqueiro, perhaps the last stanza of "Ode to a Grecian Urn" by Keats. They all offer an interrogative on art. Colinas and Cunqueiro take sculpture and painting as a motive of inspiration. Pilar Pallarés takes the word. Writing, what for?, asked Rosalía. Writing for silence?

But if the poet writes to be forgotten ("let what lived before fall into oblivion"), how does one interpret the book's final poem? Perhaps it's all a question of accepting the desire for transcendence. For art and for the word. Opposing the slate to that of Álvaro de Campos (the poem "The Tobacco Shop"). The Pessoan engineer who reflects on what has to happen and be forgotten. Everything exists for oblivion.

How difficult it is to reveal with accurate words the vast dominion that is *Book of Devorations*, so dense in its contents, so ample in perspectives, so demanding in its reading! The enormous weight of the literary and cultural tradition is evident in every verse. One cannot escape from it, and each poet must select, know how to select, their own. It is impossible to navigate several boats at once. Pilar Pallarés knows, we believe she has always known, how to select her own. A sailboat that is not lost over the horizon. Hers is a poetry with voice (voice from the word – to recreate the title of the anthology Luciano Rodríguez published years ago).

One of the most impassioned literary experiences of our time, Pilar Pallarés inscribes herself in that group of poets that posterity reveals without question.

Miguel Mato Fondo

READ MORE GALICIAN POETRY IN ENGLISH

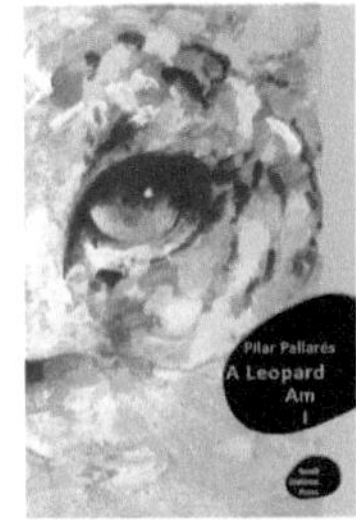

from Pilar Pallarés, *A Leopard Am I*:

Here I am, merciless, coming back to myself again,
still a Lady Lazarus,
a quivering mouth demanding nourishment
from beyond myself.
Should I hate you, now that my very quick
does not suffice?
It is you, after all, who are returning – my loss,
my amputated arm that already hurts.
True, your face is not the same and there's a change
in the contours of your body,
so much my own that I barely recognize it now as mine,
I, distinguished and powerful,
dead, in possession of myself.
You should know that I cannot give you what you need.
Don't believe in my smile – I have no claws,
no teeth,
no avid tongue sating itself with life.
I may be pale and tepid in your eyes,
but it was I
– the captive –
who cut down the garden's blooms
and who plugged the springs, immuring herself
in a naked chamber.

You ask that I be a fountain –
and I am thirst.

Translated from Galician by Carys Evans-Corrales

ISBN: 978-954-384-018-2

from Manuel Rivas, *From Unknown to Unknown*:

BALLAD ON THE WESTERN BEACHES

The ship settles on the shore
and land birds nest on its mast.
With the compass I trace routes on maps of tillage,
hurt by the sky's anger on the seed's weak ribs,
fearful of the flower's drift before inhumane winds.
The ship sleeps on the shore,
the keel's blue imagination covered in brush and rushes,
and the figurehead has a strolling soul.
In the binnacle is kept the book of moons and the rains' needle,
a bottle of old snow liqueur.
A skylark sings on a rusty harpoon,
a blackbird's sigh lashes the cables
and crows on the rudder glimpse lesser death lying alongside.
All set, admiral, for the great journey.

Translated from Galician by Jonathan Dunne

ISBN: 978-954-384-068-7

from Martín Veiga, *Jewels in the Mud: Selected Poems 1990-2020*:

THE GLEAM OF BLOOD

I saw in your smile today my mother's smile,
the same bright lift at the corners
of your mouth, the crease in the lips
that tells the punchline,
the light that softens her gaze in the
swift moment she shows surprise;
it only lasted a second,
but as the turn of the lighthouse
crossing the waters at dawn
of a dull winter lights
the empty rooms of the house,
so the gains today defeat the loss,
the gleam of blood fluttered in the cobalt
of your eyes, in your sweet smile

Translated from Galician by Keith Payne

ISBN: 978-954-384-112-7

For a full list of our publications,
please visit www.smallstations.com

www.ingramcontent.com/pod-product-compliance
Ingram Content Group UK Ltd.
Pitfield, Milton Keynes, MK11 3LW, UK
UKHW040032200726
13854UKWH00001B/480

9 789543 841134